MW01076932

10 Medicinal Mushrooms

Alison Caldwell-Andrews, PhD

Copyright © 2019 Alison Caldwell-Andrews, PhD

All rights reserved.

ISBN: 9781075218248

DEDICATION

For Greg Halliday

May you continue to light a spark in every heart you encounter
And may your good influence mushroom in all our lives.

CONTENTS

Introduction   7

1   Lion's Mane   14

2   Mesima   18

3   Turkey Tail   22

4   Shiitake   27

5   Chaga   31

6   Maitake   35

7   Tremella   40

8   Reishi   44

9   Agaricus blazei   47

10   Cordyceps   50

INTRODUCTION

Wow! Mushrooms are so good for you!

As I write this, I'm sitting next to an unopened, but labeled box. The box is a present for my birthday and it's from my thoughtful son and daughter-in-law. I can tell by the label that it's a mushroom growing kit. I'm amazed at how serendipitous it is to receive this particular gift on the very day I start writing about mushrooms. They had no idea I was even thinking about mushrooms!

Mushrooms have a long history of medicinal use. Hippocrates recommended them for their healthful qualities, both for their anti-inflammatory effects, and for their usefulness in cauterizing wounds. However, many other ancient Western healers did not appreciate mushrooms. Their attitudes toward mushrooms likely influenced the general cultural disdain for mushrooms that remains in the cultural West today (the term for this is "mycophobic"). This distaste had an unfortunate result: Western cultures did not learn to take advantage of the nutritious and medicinal qualities of mushrooms. In the East, however, mushrooms were and continue to be highly valued ("mycophilic") and widely used, not only in medicinal preparations but also in cuisine.

We see mushrooms in the grocery store or we spy them sprouting from trees or grass as we take our daily walks. Perhaps you see them in a stir fry at a restaurant. You might view them with aversion at your friend's house and, curling up your lip, you might pick them out of the casserole.

Believe it or not, you and I have more in common with a mushroom than we do with plants. On the cellular level, fungi and animals have more in common than animals and plants. So, even if you don't like eating mushrooms, you have more of an affinity for them than you may have previously assumed!

Outside of casseroles or grocery stores, identifying mushrooms is a fine art that often requires microscopic examination. It is very difficult. Variables that are examined include: color, spore print (what powdery pattern comes up when you press a mushroom onto paper) juice, bruising patterns, odor, taste, habitat, season and maturity of the mushroom. In general, leave the identification to the experts, as mistakes can be fatal. Although many mushrooms are very healthful, some are poisonous.

Mushrooms don't just pop into existence. Just like tomatoes don't pop into existence: they grow on a tomato plant. Mushrooms also grow on a support network. This support network is called the mycelium.

Mycelium is to mushrooms somewhat like what soil is to a tomato plant. It's the substrate on which mushrooms grow. Mycelium is a white, fibrous, filament network. You might compare it to millions of little threads that branch into their surroundings. You've probably seen the miracle of mycelium here and there without recognizing what it is — that fuzzy white stuff that you might notice under logs. Mycelium can be extensive. There's one report of a 2400-acre continuous mycelium network that existed in Oregon.

Mycelium can also be so small you might not even see it. Not all mycelium grows mushrooms, but all mushrooms grown on mycelium.

Mycelium can stretch through soil like webbing, holding soil together. If you've broken up soil while gardening, you have probably broken up some mycelium networks.[1] Mycelium helps decompose plant material, releases carbon dioxide into the atmosphere, increases water retention and the nutrient efficiency of plants, protects the area from pathogens and provides a food source for worms and other soil invertebrates. Mycelia eradicate pollutants, filter toxins, binds soil together, and decays organic waste. Mushrooms that grow on mycelium are a product of the nutrients gathered by that mycelium. Basically, mycelium is a way to convert organic matter into food.

Mycelium is more than simply fuzz, and it isn't always limited to a small space. This fibrous network constantly grows outward in its search for water and nutrients, provide mushrooms with sources for their nutritious value. Mycelium can grow under logs, on trees, on grass, and in soil. All these places can grow different varieties of mushrooms.

Tomato plants use roots and leaves to extract nutrients from the environment around them. Likewise, mycelium extracts nutrients from its surrounding environment. Tomatoes are the "fruiting body" of the tomato plant; mushrooms are the fruiting body of the mycelium. Tomatoes have seeds within them that are meant to grow more tomatoes; mushrooms contain spores that are meant to grow more mushrooms.

Understanding the mycelium network that mushrooms grow on is a path to understanding how useful mushrooms can be. They aren't simply a patch of diseased wood like many people think. They can be nature's little miracles, in many cases more than nutritious, and in some cases, medicinal.

---

[1] The current thinking on this is that it's better to not garden by tilling the soil (breaking it up) because mycelium not only helps decompose leaves, bark, etc., but it also helps keep moisture in the soil, prevents erosion and, entangling itself among plant roots, provides nourishment for plants.

This book focuses on medicinal mushrooms, but even the very common button mushrooms are great for you. Like all mushrooms, they are high in protein and fiber, B vitamins and minerals. Mushrooms in general contain healthy levels of anti-inflammatory compounds and anti-oxidants. Mushrooms are also known as a source of vitamin D because they can absorb significant amounts of vitamin D from the sun. Most of the vitamin D in mushrooms is in the form of D2, a form that while useful, appears to be somewhat inferior to D3 in terms of helping the human body maintain appropriate levels of vitamin D.

About half of all mushrooms are classified as "functional foods" which means that they have a net benefit to the body's health that is above and beyond their basic nutritional value. They improve the immune system, nurture the gut biome, reduce inflammation, and promote longevity. Studies show they may help aging adults to preserve cognitive abilities.[2]

A huge scientific focus in current mushroom research is the compelling anti-cancer potential for mushrooms. Although a discussion of cancer research is beyond the focus of this book, this valuable research has spurred interest in other kinds of mushroom's health benefits. For example, connected to cancer research is the scientific interest in mushroom's beta-glucan content.

Beta-glucan is a component of all mushrooms as it is one of the substances that make up a mushroom's cell walls. Beta-glucan is a polysaccharide (a complex carbohydrate) and has been linked to a wide variety of health benefits. Not only has it been shown to be highly effective in destroying various cancer cells and in helping with various cancer-related health problems, beta glucans have many other benefits.

Beta-glucans are "immunomodulators", meaning that they interact with the immune system in such a way that sets off a chain of immune-promoting events. For example, they help the immune cells communicate with one another. They stimulate the release of macrophages and lymphocytes which kill invading pathogens, tumors and viruses. Beta glucans also help balance blood lipids,

---

[2] J Tradit Complement Med. 2013 Jan-Mar; 3(1): 62–68.

therefore promoting better cardiovascular health, and they have been shown to be effective against antibiotic-resistant bacteria and viruses.

Take care, though, to remember that beta-glucan content is only one part of the mushroom. There are many other components (e.g., alpha-glucans, ergothioneines, antioxidants, anti-inflammatory sterols, lipids, glycosides, and mycoflavonoids, etc.) that have powerful effects on human health, particularly when they are all together as they are found in whole mushrooms.

The ten mushrooms in this book are each well known medicinal mushrooms. They are safe and non-toxic and have been used for thousands of years. This book will help you better understand each of these individual mushrooms and see how they can be of benefit to you. As you learn a few things about each mushroom, you will begin to see the power that mushrooms contain in terms of their impact on our overall health.

Finally, it's important to note that the many attributes listed below each mushroom in the next 10 chapters are not an exhaustive list of that mushroom's benefits. That is, I haven't listed every single benefit that exists. I have listed just some of the advantages to ingesting each of these ten wonderful mushrooms.

One thing you will notice is that these medicinal mushrooms all have some very similar effects to each other. The similar effects are in part due to the high beta-glucan content of mushrooms, and in part due to other components. The major themes include:

1. These mushrooms are all immunomodulating. This means that they help the immune system work better. (This does not mean that they "boost" or "over-activate" the immune system.)

2. These mushrooms help lower blood glucose and increase insulin sensitivity. More stable blood glucose helps the body and particularly helps the brain to work better.

3. These mushrooms provide protection for the nervous system. They nourish neurons and, in many cases,

have been found to improve cognitive health.

4. Every one of these mushrooms has been studied more for their anti-cancer qualities than any other health benefit. A discussion of this vast literature is beyond the scope of this book, but important to remember.

On the next page is a table listing the botanical name for each of the mushrooms in this book. If you want to research them further, you can get better specific information by using the botanical name. This way you can get specific information about the species by searching under the genus and species name instead of the common name that might bring up results that aren't about the same species you are looking for. So, for example, if you wanted to research shiitake mushrooms, you could use the name "L. edodes" or "Lentinula edodes" instead of "shiitake mushroom". I'll help you get used to the botanical names by interspersing them in each chapter, so you can see them next to the common name.

COMMON NAME	BOTANICAL NAME
LION'S MANE	HERICIUM ERINACEUS
MESIMA	PHELLINUS LINTEUS
TURKEY TAIL	TRAMETES VERSICOLOR
SHIITAKE	LENTINULA EDODES
CHAGA	INONOTUS OBLIQUUS
MAITAKE	GRIFOLA FRONDOSA
TREMELLA	TREMELLA FUCIFORMIS
CORDYCEPS	OPHIOCORDYCEPS SINENSIS
REISHI	GANODERMA LUCIDUM
AGARICUS	AGARICUS BLAZEI

1. LION'S MANE

The scientific name for Lion's Mane mushroom is Hericium erinaceus. Other common names include: monkey head, pom pom mushroom, bearded tooth mushroom and bearded hedgehog mushroom. There are several types of Hericium species. The H. erinaceus species is the one with most of the scientific research and use. H. erinaceus is native to Asia, however there is another similar species of Hericium (called Hericium americanum) that is native to the United States. H. americanum looks fairly similar to H. erinaceus and may have many of the same medicinal benefits. These mushrooms are safe to hunt for in the woods since there are no dangerous look-alikes and Lion's mane mushrooms are very distinct looking.

Lion's mane mushrooms generally grow on dead, decaying or wounded hardwood but also are found on other woods and can even be grown on sawdust. (Since the mycelium environment gathers nutrients from its surroundings, a less nutrient dense substrate may likely produce mushrooms that differ in nutritional value from those grown in a nutrient-rich habitat.) Lion's mane mushrooms are said to taste somewhat like crabmeat or scallops, and thus are highly prized as a food item as well as for their medicinal value. Some Asian cooks substitute these mushrooms for pork in their vegetarian dishes.

Here's why Lion's Mane is so highly valued medicinally:

1. Lion's Mane has been shown to improve mild cognitive impairment. In one study of thirty 50-80-year-old Japanese men and women with mild cognitive impairment, the intervention group took 1000 mgs of Lion's Mane three times per day and the placebo group took a placebo. After eight weeks, the intervention group performed significantly better on tests of cognitive dysfunction. They continued to improve at weeks 12 and 16 (at which time they stopped taking Lion's Mane). In other words, the longer they took the mushrooms, the more improvement they saw. However, these observable benefits disappeared after about a month of not taking the mushrooms.[3]

2. Lion's Mane mushrooms contain a compound called erinacine, which has been shown to increase a substance called Nerve Growth Factor (NGF). NGF improves nerve cell survival during stroke and reduces amyloid-β plaque in

---

[3] Phytother Res. 2009 Mar;23(3):367-72

the brain. NGF helps nerve cells to function properly, repair themselves and to communicate with the rest of the nervous system. It is thought that the compounds in Lion's Mane that increase NGF can pass through the blood-brain barrier unlike other sources of NGF.

3. Erinacine is a compound found in H. erinaceus that has been well-studied for its medicinal value. Much of that study involves anti-cancer research. Erinacine is also significantly anti-inflammatory. Amyloid-β plaque is an inflammatory protein fragment that accumulates in the brain, destroying nerve synapses and causing nerve cell death in the case of Alzheimer's disease. Erinacine helps destroy these inflammatory plaques, resulting in significant help for Alzheimer's patients.[4]

4. Erinacine also showed some potential (in a rat study) for healing dopaminergic lesions and reducing the oxidative stress in the brain that is found in Parkinson's disease.[5]

5. Lion's Mane can reduce depression[6]. This mushroom helps regulate (and enhance) the production of BDNF (brain derived neurotrophic factor). BDNF is important in creating new nerve cells, nourishing nerve cells and

---

[4] Behav Neurol. 2018; 2018: 5802634.
[5] ibid
[6] J Agric Food Chem. 2015 Aug 19;63(32):7108-23.

improving mood. Lion's Mane's also can modulate certain neurotransmitters (MAO's) and reduce inflammation. This ability, in combination with BDNF increases, partly explains how Lion's Mane can reduce depression. Two grams per day for 4 weeks was shown to significantly affect depression.[7]

6. Lion's mane mushrooms help myelinate neurons. Myelin is the fatty "sheath" or covering that helps nerve communication happen faster. Myelination also helps support and nourish the nerve cells. There are compounds in Lion's Mane that help not myelinate, but also help re-stimulate myelin production after damage has occurred.[8]

7. Hericium erinaceus (see, I switched to the botanical name to help you get used to it) is also known for helping manage blood sugar AND blood lipids (like triglycerides and cholesterol). In addition, Lion's mane protects the liver. [9]

8. H. erinaceus improves anxiety.[10]

9. H. erinaceus also blocks a particular kind of pain signaling (specifically ATP-induced Ca^{2+} signaling in human HOS cells). This function results in significant reductions in neuropathic pain[11] and other kinds of pain (including ulcer pain).

10. Lion's mane also helps with stomach problems: pancreatitis, Crohn's disease, hemorrhoids, nausea.

---

[7] Journal of Restorative Medicine, Volume 6, Number 1, 12 March 2017, pp. 19-26(8)
[8] Fiziol Zh. 2003;49(1):38-45.
[9] Int J Biol Macromol. 2017 Apr;97:228-237
[10] J Agric Food Chem. 2015 Aug 19;63(32):7108-23.
[11] Int J Med Mushrooms. 2017;19(6):499-507

2. MESIMA

Unlike the delicate and delicious tasting Lion's Mane mushroom, the mesima, or meshima (Phellinus linteus) mushroom is bitter and quite unpleasant to taste. When ingested, it is usually taken as a medicinal tea. It remains popular despite its taste because of its outstanding medicinal qualities. It outweighs all the other mushrooms in its class for its concentration of anti-tumor properties. For example, one article that examined the combination of mesima and reishi mushrooms on the destruction of ovarian cancer called the two mushrooms a  "lethal synergy."[12] (Lethal to the cancer, not to people!)

Like Lion's mane, mesima mushrooms are native to Asia but also grow in tropical America and Africa. They are wood decay mushrooms that often grow on mulberry trees and somewhat

---

[12] Oncotarget. 2018 Jan 4;9(5):6308-6319

resemble black hooves stuck onto the tree. Hence, their nickname: The Black Hoof mushroom.

Traditionally, the Chinese used mesima to relieve gut discomfort and gastrointestinal pain and treat chronic diarrhea. It was also used to help stop bleeding (including excessive menstrual bleeding and bleeding from the ovaries) and to treat arthritis.

Here are some reasons why mesima mushrooms are valued:

1. Mesima mushrooms have anti-inflammatory and antioxidant effects. Mesima mushrooms inhibit the expression of a variety of pro-inflammatory compounds (including nitric oxide) and a variety of different pro-inflammatory signaling pathways. Mesima mushrooms also demonstrate excellent anti-aging activity due to increasing antioxidant defenses and by decreasing the oxidative stress that causes aging. [13]

2. Mesima mushrooms have immunomodulatory effects. In general, mushrooms modulate the immune system but do not overstimulate, over-activate or "boost" the immune system. Mesima mushrooms promote immune activity (for example, increasing the number of immune cells available). Mesima mushrooms also help manage inflammation. They are labeled as "strong" immunomodulatory agents. Remember, modulating the immune system strengthens immunity but is not the same thing as "boosting" (over-activating) the immune system. What you're looking for is a well-regulated and responsive immune system that is strong, not one that has been "boosted."[14]

3. Phellinus linteus (the botanical name for mesima) show anti-allergic effects. P. linteus appears to have good potential to help reduce allergic activity in reactions that are related to IgE.[15] IgE is the antibody that causes the body's reactions to the allergen.

---

[13] Molecules. 2019 May; 24(10): 1888.
[14] Ibid
[15] Food Sci Biotechnol. 2017 Apr 30;26(2):467-472.

4. P. linteus also has antimicrobial and antiviral effects. P. linteus shows "potent" antimicrobial activity against both staph (S. aureus) and MRSA.[16] P. linteus also is effective against the virus Influenza A H5N1 and against H1N1.

5. Mesima mushrooms have antidiabetic effects. Not only does the mesima mushroom increase the production of insulin in damaged cells, it also reduces the pro-inflammatory cells that are responsible for autoimmune type diabetes. Mesima decreases blood glucose and increases glucose tolerance. Thus, there are multiple pathways in which mesima mushrooms can reduce diabetes.[17]

6. Mesima mushrooms have hepatoprotective effects. P. linteus protects against hepatic fibrosis[18] which is abnormally large amounts of scar tissue that builds up in the liver when it attempts to repair itself. The scarring is not

---

[16] Bioorg Med Chem Lett. 2011 Mar 15;21(6):1716-8
[17] Molecules. 2019 May; 24(10): 1888.
[18] Molecules. 2018 Jul 12;23(7). pii: E1705.

much of an issue by itself, but it leaves the liver vulnerable to diseases such as cirrhosis.

7. Neuroprotective effects are of interest in medicinal mushrooms and P. linteus does not disappoint! One way in which mesima mushrooms protect the brain is through their potent antioxidant activity. Specifically, they reduce ROS (reactive oxygen species: unstable, oxidized cells that run amok destroying neurons).

8. Mesima mushrooms show cardioprotective (heart) effects. A compound, hispidin, found in mesima mushrooms protects heart muscle cells (specifically the cells that grow into heart muscle cells), preventing cell death resulting from oxidation.[19]

9. Hispidin also protects pancreatic cells from oxidation.[20] These protected cells also showed an increase in insulin production, creating an anti-diabetic effect and showing the potential for mesima mushrooms to reduce the oxidative damage that results from diabetes.

10. Mesima mushrooms show gastroprotective effects. A study examined the protective effect of P. linteus compounds on gastric ulcers induced by the NSAID naproxen. P. linteus was able to protect the gut from damage caused by NSAID use.[21]

---

[19] Exp Cell Res. 2014 Oct 1;327(2):264-75
[20] J Med Food. 2011 Nov;14(11):1431-8.
[21] J Microbiol Biotechnol. 2016 May 28;26(5):823-8

3. TURKEY TAIL

Turkey tail (Trametes versicolor[22]) mushrooms are one of the more common mushrooms you'll find in the forest, and they can be found the world over. They grow on almost any type of wood. They break down dead wood and help return those nutrients to the soil.

Like other mushrooms they have mostly been used by Asian cultures. The Chinese call them "cloud fungus" and the Japanese call them "mushroom by the riverbank." (It is true, there are no wild turkeys in Japan or China but there are plenty of clouds and rivers.)

Although they are edible, they are not going to feature themselves in your cuisine. They are tough and leathery and not very tasty. It is best to dry them and then grind the dried mushrooms into a powder to use to make tea. They can also be steeped in alcohol to make an extraction. Incidentally, steeping in hot water and soaking in alcohol result in extracting differing medicinal

---

[22] Note that these mushrooms are also known by the names Coriolis versicolor and Polyporus versicolr as synonyms to Trametes versicolor

compounds in almost all plants and mushrooms.

Here are some reasons to love turkey tail mushrooms:

1. Turkey tail mushrooms are high in antioxidants. Oxidation causes cellular damage. Antioxidants help prevent damage by neutralizing free radicals. Antioxidants also reduce inflammation.

2. Turkey tail mushrooms are primarily known for two polysaccharopeptides that are known as PSK (krestin) and PSP (polysaccharide peptide). Much research has been done on how PSK and PSP can destroy cancer cells. They also help with general immune functioning. PSP increases the number of white blood cells that fight infection. PSK stimulates cells that protect against toxins and helps activate macrophages (specialized immune cells that consume invaders like bacteria and virus cells).

3. Turkey tail mushrooms also improve gut health by suppressing the growth of harmful bacteria that occur after

administration of antibiotics (like e. coli and shigella). They also nourish recovery through prebiotic nutrition.[23] PSP extracted from turkey tail mushrooms is shown to significantly increase levels of health-promoting gut bacteria including Bifidobacterium spp., Lactobacillus spp. These mushrooms also reduced harmful varieties of gut bacteria, including Clostridium spp., Staphylococcus spp. and Enterococcus spp.[24]

4. Trametes versicolor (botanical name again) also decreases insulin resistance and lowers blood sugar. The changes in gene and protein expression that occurred after use of turkey tail mushroom were described as "remarkable anti-insulin-resistance effects." [25]

5. The word "ergogenic" means enhancing physical performance, stamina or recovery. Athletes love ergogenic foods. Turkey tail mushrooms are ergogenic (as shown in a mouse study). Not only do turkey tail mushrooms appear to reduce fatigue, but they may also lower blood lactate levels after exercise, thus promoting more energy. Elevated blood ammonia levels can cause increased fatigue; these mushrooms may lower blood ammonia levels after exercise. Trametes versicolor improved the use of blood glucose and resulted in lower blood glucose after exercise as compared to placebo.[26]

6. ALP (alkaline phosphatase) is an enzyme that the liver uses to break down proteins. When ALP levels are high, there is potential for liver damage. Turkey tail mushroom lowers ALP levels. Liver cells also release ALT (alanine transaminase) enzymes when damaged. Turkey tail mushrooms lower levels of ALT.[27]

7. Traditional Chinese medicine used turkey tail mushroom as a treatment for chronic hepatitis, upper respiratory infections, urinary infections, digestive tract infections and

[23] Gut Microbes. 2014 Jul 1;5(4):458-67.
[24] Plant Foods Hum Nutr. 2013 Jun;68(2):107-12
[25] Phytother Res. 2018 Mar;32(3):551-560
[26] Int J Med Sci. 2017; 14(11): 1110–1117.
[27] Int J Med Sci. 2017; 14(11): 1110–1117.

to help with the immune system. [28]

One final note for fun:

The turkey tail mushroom is a gorgeous mushroom. Looking at it you would never use the words "white rot fungi" to describe it, yet that's technically what it is. White rot fungi are all the fungi that help decompose wood (cell walls and lignans) and leave the decayed wood looking whitish in color.

The reason I'm bringing this up is because turkey tail mushrooms have a really cool commercial application that depends on them being a white rot fungus. They are used to help purify hospital

---

[28] Int J Med Sci. 2017; 14(11): 1110–1117.

wastewater. Hospital waste is full of pharmacologically active compounds. Turkey tail mushrooms are very good at degrading (cleansing) these compounds: results show that in the current waste management design, they can remove 70% of the pharmacological compounds.[29] This should give you a good idea about how powerful these mushrooms can be in terms of helping your body become healthier too.

---

[29] J Biol Eng. 2019 May 29;13:47.

4. SHIITAKE

The Japanese word "také" means "mushroom." That's why you see it in the names for two mushrooms: shiitake and maitake (Chapter 6), both powerful medicinal mushrooms. The prefix "shii" in shiitake is the name of the tree that shiitake mushrooms originally grew on. (The prefix "mai" means "dance" and you'll see that in the chapter on maitake mushrooms.)

However, since shiitakes are now the second most commonly cultivated edible mushroom, you can find them worldwide and not just growing on "shii". They have a meaty texture and what is described as a smoky or earthy taste. They are very popular in Asian cuisine and becoming more widely used in North America. Originally from Japan, 80% of them are now grown in China.

Shiitake (Lentinula edodes) is a variety of mushroom that should be fully cooked before eating due to an allergy called shiitake dermatitis. This problem is rare as only 2% of people who eat these mushrooms undercooked or raw develop this non-fatal allergic reaction. Nonetheless, cook your shiitake mushrooms to 300° F (145 ° C).

Here are some of things that make shiitake mushrooms special:

1. One of the specific beta-glucans found in shiitake mushrooms is Lentinan, which has been shown to act powerfully in the immune system. One of the things Lentinan does to help immunity is that it enhances the ability of macrophages (immune cells) to kill invader cells. This beta-glucan, Lentinan also enhances T-cell activity and NK (natural killer cells) cell activity, two other types of immune cells.[30] Most research on Lentinan has been done in the area of cancer treatment.

2. Lentinan is effective against viruses, bacterial infections and parasitic infection, and it has been shown to inhibit HIV. Other components of the shiitake mushroom (water soluble lignans and Centinamycins) also help destroy viruses and bacteria.[31]

3. Another medicinal effect of shiitake is its antioxidant capacity. Oxidized blood lipids are closely linked to heart disease. The European Food Safety Association recommends beta-glucan rich and phytosterol rich

---

[30] Sci Rep. 2017; 7: 1314.
[31] J Tradit Complement Med. 2012 Apr-Jun; 2(2): 84–95.

functional foods (remember, these are foods that provide benefits that exceed their mere nutritional content, and shiitake is a functional food) can reduce oxidation as well as reduce blood lipid levels. for helping reduce cardiovascular disease. Shiitake mushrooms are rich in both beta glucan and phytosterol, both compounds with antioxidant effects. Some of the food components of L. edodes, like vitamin E, fatty acids and butyric acid, also act against atherosclerosis. The antioxidant effects of shiitake mushrooms act on the body both in general ways and specifically on oxidized lipids.[32]

4. Lentinula edodes (botanical name for shiitake) has been shown to quickly adsorb the dangerous heavy metal, cadmium, from gastrointestinal fluid, making these mushrooms useful for cadmium detoxification.[33]

5. Shiitake mushrooms are anti-inflammatory in general, and specifically anti-inflammatory for the gut. They can reduce intestinal inflammation and therefore may be useful in the treatment of inflammatory bowel disease (IBD).[34]

6. Shiitake mushrooms can powerfully help the immune system. One demonstration of this is the capacity of these mushrooms to heal atopic dermatitis.[35] One study examined college students whose immunity (especially gut immunity) improved after 4 weeks of regular shiitake mushroom eating.[36]

7. An animal study looked at rats who were on a high fat diet. Some rats were given more shiitake mushrooms in their diet and others received less. The rats with high shiitake mushroom levels in their diet showed lower weight gain and lower fat deposits as compared to rats on lower amounts of shiitake. Blood triglycerides were also lower in the rats with the high shiitake mushroom addition to their diet.[37]

---

[32] Saudi J Biol Sci. 2018 Dec; 25(8): 1515–1523.
[33] Int J Environ Res Public Health. 2014 Dec 1;11(12):12486-98
[34] PLoS One. 2013 Apr 22;8(4):e62441
[35] Molecules. 2016 Jul 29;21(8)
[36] J Am Coll Nutr. 2015;34(6):478-87

8. Shiitake mushrooms can benefit dental health. The word that is used in the literature is a great example of "medical jargon": anticariogenicity, which simply means anti-cavity-growing. Shiitake mushrooms can stop dental decay due to cavities. Volunteers in a study were asked to rinse their mouths with a solution containing shiitake mushrooms. Results showed that L. edodes reduced cavities. Shiitake boosts dental health through the following paths: a) compounds in the mushroom protect the dental enamel from cavity-creating bacteria, b) shiitake compounds change how dental surfaces interact with moisture, including disrupting bacteria laden biofilms that promote tooth decay c) shiitake compounds kill bacteria and d) they disrupt the functioning of a particularly damaging dental pathogen, *Streptococcus mutans.*[38] [39]

9. L. edodes are rich in B vitamins which help with liver function and with brain function.

[37] J Obes. 2011; 2011: 258051.
[38] Pharmacogn Rev. 2016 Jul-Dec; 10(20): 100–104.
[39] BMC Complement Altern Med. 2013 May 29;13:117

5. CHAGA

Chaga (Inonotus obliquus) mushrooms almost all grow on the bark of birch trees, but can also be found on poplar, oak and beech in the cold climate areas of Europe, Russia, Siberia, Korea, Alaska, the Adirondack mountains in the USA, and in Northern Canada.

Inonotus obliquus are not attractive: they look like a pile of burnt charcoal with an orange soft inside. This look is not lost in the common names for chaga mushrooms which include: black mass, clinker polypore (clinker is the name for slag left over from a coal fire), birch canker polypore, and cinder conk.

Fried cinder conk, anyone? Anyone? Or maybe a birch canker?

Yeah, no one fries it for breakfast or for any other meal. It's traditionally ground into a powder and made into a medicinal tea. Happily, it tastes better than you might think upon looking at it. It has a somewhat earthy taste with hints of vanilla (and no hints of burnt charcoal).[40] Indigenous Siberians have used Chaga mushrooms for thousands of years. The fungus grows on hardwood trees in places where the tree wood has been injured. It's like a protective scar for the tree and the tree can continue to live for decades with chaga mushroom growths all over it.

There is a story that the Grand Prince of old Russia, Tsar Valdimir Monomakh, used Chaga to cure his lip cancer in the 1100's. Many centuries later, the famed Soviet author, Solzhenitsyn, described it thus: "He could not imagine any greater joy than to go away into the woods for months on end, to break off this chaga, crumble it, boil it up on a campfire, drink it and get well like an animal" (Cancer Ward, 1968).

These stories make some of the other names for chaga make more sense: Gift from God, Mushroom of Immortality, and Diamond of the Forest.[41] These names are based in the action of the mushroom rather than its looks, and certainly sound more appealing!

Like the previous mushrooms, chaga is known for immunomodulatory action, lowering blood sugar, anti-

---

[40] http://www.ethnoherbalist.com/chaga-extract-mushroom-tea-benefits/
[41] Molecules. 2013 Aug; 18(8): 9293–9304.

inflammatory benefits and lowering cholesterol. The black color of chaga is due to the large amounts of the pigment melanin.
Following are reasons to use chaga mushrooms:

1. The melanin in chaga mushrooms is not only a pigment and a potent antioxidant, but also has a beneficial effect on gut health by promoting the growth of the gut bacteria, *Bifidobacterium bifidum* [42] (Here's another word for you: Bifidogenesis: promotion of Bifidobacterium growth).

2. Chaga is antibiotic. Since all mushrooms, chaga included, must regularly defend themselves against bacteria, they all have good antibiotic qualities.

3. Chaga mushrooms may protect against Alzheimer's disease by modulating key signaling pathways that prevent cell death.[43] The word for preventing cell death is "antiapoptotic," in case you want to stump your family![44]

4. Chaga also protects the brain through its antioxidant activity.

5. Chaga appears to be helpful for diabetes. Some of the polysaccharides in chaga were shown to decrease insulin resistance in vitro, raising cells' abilities to absorb glucose. Chaga's ability to lower blood glucose and increase insulin sensitivity outperformed the popular anti-diabetic drug, Metformin, in this study.[45]

6. Chaga mushrooms can effectively reduce damaging inflammation and are a potentially valuable treatment for inflammatory bowel diseases (IBD) such as colitis.[46] A mouse study showed the potential of these mushrooms for helping reduce inflammation and healing chronic pancreatitis.[47]

---

[42] Biomolecules. 2019 Jun 24;9(6). pii: E248
[43] Int J Biol Macromol. 2019 Jun 15;131:769-778
[44] Or if you just want to sound like a serious nerd!
[45] Molecules. 2018 Dec; 23(12): 3261.
[46] J Ethnopharmacol. 2012 Sep 28;143(2):524-32
[47] Int J Biol Macromol. 2016 Jun;87:348-56.

7. Sometimes, in the normal healing response to infection, the body overproduces certain chemicals that accelerate inflammation. Inflammation is critical to healing, but too much is problematic. Chaga exerts much of its anti-inflammatory action by appropriately suppressing proinflammatory mediators (like NO, or nitric oxide, COX-2, TNF-α, IL-1β, and IL-6).[48] This suppression does not mean that Chaga interferes with healing or that chaga suppresses the immune system. Rather, this is an example of "modulating" the immune system.

8. Based on in vitro experiments (not a human study), chaga mushrooms appear to perform better than the popular minoxidil for promoting hair growth.[49] This may be why traditional Asian cultures have used chaga mushrooms as a hair shampoo.

9. Chaga mushrooms may relieve pain. "Nociceptive" is a word that means "pain". One animal study showed "anti-nociceptive" potential as well as anti-inflammatory effects of chaga.[50] However, this has not yet been well studied in humans.

10. Finally, these mushrooms may also help with fatigue. In a mouse study, mice who consumed chaga mushrooms had extended swim times as well as higher glycogen (energy) levels in the muscle and liver. Blood levels of lactic acid and urea nitrogen levels were decreased, also supporting an anti-fatigue effect.[51]

[48] Molecules. 2013 Aug; 18(8): 9293–9304.
[49] J Nat Med. 2019 Jun;73(3):597-601.
[50] J Ethnopharmacol. 2005 Oct 3;101(1-3):120-8.
[51] J Tradit Chin Med. 2015 Aug;35(4):468-72.

6. MAITAKE

The botanical name Grifola frondosa is almost whimsical and is certainly in contrast to the popular name "black mass" for chaga that you saw in the last chapter. This beautiful, floral-like mushroom is nicknamed The Dancing Mushroom ("mai" means "dance" in Japanese), and in addition to inspiring mushroom hunters to dance with joy, maitake has excellent health benefits.

Originating in, and most common in both Japan and North America, maitake mushrooms have made their way around the world. In Northeast American, you can find them in the fall, at the base of oak trees (and sometimes maple or elm).

In England, they are primarily known as "hen of the woods."[52] This nickname is also common in America, as is another nickname:

---

[52] Not to be confused with "chicken of the woods" which is a different mushroom

"sheepshead." These mushrooms are said to have a delicious flavor reminiscent of chicken and are widely used in Japanese cooking. Italians call it signorina (their word for an unmarried woman, like the title "miss"). Because it can grow to a weight of 20 kilograms (between 40-50 lbs.), the Japanese call it King of the Mushrooms.

Here are some reasons you'll want to include maitake mushrooms in your mushroom routine:

1. Like all the other mushrooms detailed in this book, maitake are prized for their beta-glucan content. Beta glucan is the mushroom component that is responsible for maitake's "non-specific" immunomodulator effect, which means that the ability of maitake, and all other mushrooms in this book, to fight infection is not limited to any specific type of infection.

2. Maitake has anti-viral and anti-microbial properties in addition to increasing the body's ability to use the immune system to fight invaders.

3. Maiitake's ability to increase the number of immune cells called macrophages is particularly impressive.

4. Maitake is unique compared to other mushrooms because the way the beta-glucan are structured (they call this "branching") in maitake differs from most mushrooms.[53] [54] One result of this structure finding yielded the creation of two patented compounds called D-fraction and MD-fraction, both of which have been studied for their anti-cancer properties. They help in helping prevent metastasis, slowing or stopping tumor growth and protecting healthy cells so they do not become cancerous.

5. Some researchers have considered maitake to be an adaptogen, citing positive benefits on chronic fatigue syndrome as well as on vaginal yeast overgrowth (candida albicans) and uterine fibroids.[55]

6. Like other mushrooms in this book, maitake has anti-diabetic effects. It helps inhibit blood sugar from rising as well as increasing insulin sensitivity.

7. Animal studies show that maitake can lower blood pressure.

---

[53] Nerd alert: Instead of 1,3 main chain with 1,6 branches, maitake has both 1,3 and 1,6 main chains with both 1,3 and 1,6 branches. The theory is that the more branches, the higher likelihood that more immune cells will be activated.
[54] http://archive.foundationalmedicinereview.com/publications/6/1/48.pdf
[55] Ibid

8. Grifola frondosa (maitake's botanical name) has been shown to lower the body burden of mercury by adsorbing[56] this highly damaging heavy metal. These mushrooms can reduce blood levels of mercury as well as reduce mercury levels in the liver and kidneys.[57]

9. Maitake mushrooms improve cardiovascular health by reducing blood lipid levels and by inhibiting cholesterol (LDL – the "bad" cholesterol) oxidation in the liver. Maitake does this through changing how key enzymes synthesize, break down and absorb triglycerides.[58]

10. Maitake mushrooms have effects in two different immunity "divisions." Here's what this means: The immune system contains two divisions. These two divisions are known as cellular immunity and humoral immunity. Humoral immunity is named "humoral" because it involves things found in body fluids (or "humors"). Humoral immunity focuses primarily on antibodies and includes complement proteins and some antimicrobial peptides, all immune cells that are found in body fluids. Humoral immunity's main warfare stage is outside the cell. In contrast, cellular immunity's main stage is inside the cell. Cellular immunity targets infected cells and works with immune cells like macrophages and natural killer (NK) cells on the inside of the cell. Scientists have found that a combination of maitake and shiitake mushrooms have a synergistic effect when used together that more strongly stimulates both the cellular and humoral immune system divisions as compared to when these mushrooms are used alone.[59]

11. Neurite outgrowth is what happens when nerves either grow or regenerate, resulting in the growth of projections off the neuron body, called axons or dendrites. Axons and dendrites help connect neurons to other neurons. Maitake mushrooms have been shown to stimulate neurite outgrowth, resulting in better brain health. In addition to

[56] Adsorbing differs from absorbing.
[57] Sci Rep. 2018 Dec 4;8(1):17630
[58] Front Microbiol. 2016 Aug 3;7:1186
[59] Ann Transl Med. 2014 Feb;2(2):14

maitake mushrooms, other mushrooms have shown this same ability: reishi, cordyceps, tiger milk mushrooms (L. rhinocerotis) and giant oyster mushrooms (P. giganteus).[60]

12. Maitake and reishi mushrooms also contain compounds that stimulate nerve growth factor (NGF) which protects and enhances cognitive growth and function.[61]

---

[60] BMC Complement Altern Med. 2013 Oct 11;13:261.
[61] BMC Complement Altern Med. 2013 Jul 4;13:157

7. TREMELLA

Tremella fuciformis is a delicacy in Asia. Although there's not much to taste, it's the texture that is featured in tremella cuisine. Tremella is simultaneously both soft and crunchy, although that may be hard to imagine without experiencing it. It's frequently served as a dessert after being soaked in a sugared liquid, somewhat like canned peaches.

Tremella fuciformis is known most commonly as simply, tremella. Other names include beauty mushroom, silver ear, white jelly and my favorite, snow fungus.

Traditionally used in China to treat tuberculosis and high blood pressure, the medical interest at present, like other mushrooms, lies primarily in its anti-cancer properties.

Unlike many other mushrooms, tremella mushrooms do not act to decay wood. So, although they do grow on wood, they are not using the wood nutritionally. Instead, they are a kind of mushroom known as a "mycoparasite." In other words, they eat some of the other fungi that do grown on wood.

Incidentally, I have to bring an interesting mushroom that is related to Tremella fuciformis, which is the mushroom Tremella mesenterica, also known as witch's butter (there's a picture of this mushroom at the end of this chapter). Tremella mesenterica is also a mycoparasite. But honestly, I just wanted you to know that in addition to mushrooms named tiger milk (see the last chapter if you missed that one) there are also mushrooms known as witch's butter.[62]

Now, back to the main point: tremella. There are lots of other reasons to eat tremella mushrooms other than their reputation as a food delicacy. Centuries ago hardly anyone could afford them but now they are becoming more available thanks to medicinal interest.

Tremella fuciformis is a valued medicinal mushroom:

    1. Tremella mushrooms are anti-inflammatory and good anti-

---

[62] And now my work here is done

oxidants. They counteract inflammation caused by proinflammatory cytokines and ROS (reactive oxygen species that damage cells through their instability),[63] as well as countering oxidative cell death caused by hydrogen peroxide.[64]

2. Nerve damage is one result of trauma to the body. One way to treat nerve damage is through applying a nerve graft made of silicone. These "autographs" are considered "gold standard" therapy, yet they bring with them problematic disadvantages like limited availability and they don't work perfectly. Advances in this technology have led to the development of nerve conduits that are "pre-loaded" with bioactive material. The purpose of the bioactive material is to help connect the nerves more successfully. Because tremella has been shown to enhance neurite outgrowth (see chapter on maitake), it was chosen as the bioactive component on autographs in a study that examined using tremella conduits to bridge a 15 mm gap between nerves. Exciting results showed that tremella promoted peripheral nerve regeneration in both short and long term (up to 8 months).[65]

---

[63] Anal Cell Pathol (Amst). 2018; 2018: 5762371.
[64] Mol Med Rep. 2017 Aug; 16(2): 1340–1346.
[65] Evid Based Complement Alternat Med. 2013; 2013: 959261.

3. Tremella is shown to have altered and normalized diabetes-associated proteins and normalized the obesity and diabetes-associated regulatory molecules resistin and adiponectin in diabetic mice. This study indicates that tremella may help regulate gene expression in obesity and diabetes, with treatment implications for both.[66]

4. Tremella has been used in China to treat exhaustion.[67]

5. Tremella may improve impaired cognition including memory by improving neurite outgrowth.[68] These mushrooms, also through neurite outgrowth, may protect brain neurons in the case of Alzheimer's disease.[69]

6. Like the other medicinal mushrooms, tremella lowers blood sugar and cholesterol, and is immunomodulatory.[70]

7. Tremella was evaluated for safety and efficacy in a cognitive impairment study. Results showed that memory and executive functioning improved in the tremella group as compared to placebo. Participants took 1200mg/day tremella for 8 weeks. No safety concerns were found.[71]

Finally, here's that picture of Tremella mesenterica, or witch's butter:

[66] J Microbiol Biotechnol. 2009 Oct;19(10):1109-21.
[67] Evid Based Complement Alternat Med. 2013; 2013: 959261.
[68] Biol Pharm Bull. 2007 Apr;30(4):708-14.
[69] Mycobiology. 2007 Mar;35(1):11-5.
[70] Int J Biol Macromol. 2019 Jan;121:1005-1010.
[71] J Med Food. 2018 Apr;21(4):400-407

8. REISHI

Reishi mushrooms are among the more famous medicinal mushrooms. Reminiscent of a sunrise, they are gorgeous to look at and spectacular in their performance. Known in China as lingzhi, the reishi mushroom is seen by the Chinese as the ultimate in spiritual potency combined with the essence of immortality. The botanical name, Ganoderma lucidum, refers to the varnished, glossy appearance of these beauties.

Considered the top herb in traditional Chinese medicine (surpassing even ginseng), Reishi has been used for over two thousand years. Anciently, it was rare and literally worth its weight in gold, therefore only used by those few who could afford its luxury. Now, reishi is widely cultivated and easier to find. Varieties of Ganoderma grow throughout the world and you are likely to run across some in your forest hikes.

It's a tough and woody mushroom, not easy to eat nor easy to digest. Therefore, the best way to enjoy its many medicinal benefits is through extraction of the medicinal components.

Here are some of the many reasons reishi should be on anyone's list of medicinal mushrooms to use:

1. Reishi is a strong immunomodulator. It has been shown to increase the number of infection-fighting cytokines, enhance the proliferation and maturation of NK cells, T and B lymphocytes, and splenic mononuclear cells and other cells that respond to the need for immune activities (cells that respond to the immune system are called immunological effector cells).[72] [73]

2. Neurotransmitters are chemicals in the body and brain that help nerves communicate. The first neurotransmitter to be discovered was named acetylcholine. It speeds up or slows down nerve signals depending on what is needed. It plays a role in arousal, learning, memory and neuroplasticity among many other things. Damage to the cholinergic part of the brain (the part that makes acetylcholine) is linked to Alzheimer's disease. Ganoderma lucidem (botanical name) protects acetylcholine from breaking down. G. lucidem is known as an antiacetylcholinesterase[74] which means that it prevents

---

[72] A Medicinal Mushroom, Chapter 9,Ganoderma lucidum (Lingzhi or Reishi) Sissi Wachtel-Galor, John Yuen, John A. Buswell, and Iris F. F. Benzie.
[73] J Pharmacol Sci. 2005 Oct;99(2):144-53.
[74] Another word you can use around the family dinner table to impress.

destruction of acetylcholine by the enzyme acetylcholinesterase.[75]

3. Like you would expect at this point in the book, reishi is highly anti-inflammatory and is a good antioxidant.[76] A group of angina patients showed antioxidant benefits when given Polysaccharide Peptide (PSP) from Ganoderma lucidem, and reishi was considered a "potent" antioxidant.[77]

4. Reishi is antibacterial and antiviral including effects against HIV and against gram-positive bacteria.[78]

5. Reishi has been shown to help protect the liver. It protects against liver injury and against cirrhosis as well as improve liver functioning.[79]

6. Reishi also can heal gastric ulcers and restore mucus and prostaglandin levels to normal.[80]

7. Women with fibromyalgia were given reishi for 6 weeks and then measured for any potential gains in physical fitness. Results showed improved aerobic endurance, lower body flexibility, and velocity.[81]

---

[75] Molecules. 2018 Mar; 23(3): 649.
[76] Molecules. 2018 Mar; 23(3): 649.
[77] Indian Heart J. 2018 Sep - Oct;70(5):608-614.
[78] A Medicinal Mushroom, Chapter 9,Ganoderma lucidum (Lingzhi or Reishi) Sissi Wachtel-Galor, John Yuen, John A. Buswell, and Iris F. F. Benzie.
[79] ibid
[80] ibid
[81] Nutr Hosp. 2015 Nov 1;32(5):2126-35

9. AGARICUS BLAZEI

Agaricus blazei is best known by its botanical name, but it is also called the Royal Sun Agaricus. It was first discovered in Brazil and has a long history of use by natives who call it "The Mushroom of the Gods."

Brazil gave the country of Japan the gift of Agaricus blazei spores in 1965 and now Japan and other Asian countries are prolific growers of this mushroom. Agaricus blazei grows on grass rather than in the forest on trees. It is mostly cultivated on straw in commercial operations. Production has been encouraged commercially so much that it's become difficult to discriminate pure strains.

Traditional uses include common diseases like atherosclerosis, hepatitis, hyperlipidemia, diabetes, dermatitis and cancer.[82] Agaricus is less well-known as a medicinal mushroom and therefore there is less research to look at.

---

[82] J Tradit Complement Med. 2012 Apr-Jun; 2(2): 84–95.

Agaricus is also believed to fight physical and emotional stress, stimulate immune system, improve the quality of life in diabetics, reduce cholesterol, prevent osteoporosis and peptic ulcer, treat circulatory and digestive problems and fight cancer.[83]

It is used as a food as well as medicinally and has somewhat of an almond flavor.

Here are some reasons why Agaricus blazei is included as a medicinal mushroom:

1. Agaricus blazei increases the number of immune cells including cytotoxic T-cells.[84] Cells that are termed "cytotoxic" are cells that destroy invading cells. One of the ways A. blazei protects the body is by destroying potential invader cells. Incidentally, it's thought that this is one of the ways A. blazei is anti-cancer.

2. A common worry in auto-immune disease is that the immune system will be unnecessarily activated, or that activation of immune cells will result in unnecessary levels of inflammation. One type of immune cell is called a dendritic cell (DC). These cells can recognize pathogens and act against them, but they are generally inactive ("immature") until contact with pathogens "wakes them up." When this contact happens, they can become pro-inflammatory. This inflammation is intended to help rid the body of invading pathogens and if regulated can be very helpful. However, inflammation can be problematic if out of control, particularly in individuals with auto-immune disease because inflammation can worsen the autoimmune disease. One study examined Agaricus blazei's impact on these dendritic immune cells and found that A. blazei could activate DC cells without setting off pro-inflammatory actions by the DC cells. This type of activation or maturation differed from the activation caused by pathogenic cells, thereby inhibiting what might be unnecessary inflammation.[85]

---

[83] Evid Based Complement Alternat Med. 2008 Mar; 5(1): 3–15.
[84] Biosci Biotechnol Biochem. 1998 Mar;62(3):434-7.
[85] Immunology. 2005 Mar; 114(3): 397–409.

3. A. blazei lowers blood pressure, both systolic and diastolic.[86]

4. A. blazei lowered blood serum values for the Hepatitis C[87] virus.

5. A. blazei appears to reduce weight and lower cholesterol in some patients.[88]

6. A. blazei protects brain tissue from oxidation and promotes mitochondrial activity in the brain.[89]

7. Acetaminophen can cause injury to both brain tissue and liver tissue. One study showed that pretreatment using A. blazei protected brain tissue and liver tissue from damage by acetaminophen.[90]

8. An animal study in aging rats found that Agaricus blazei helped preserve the myenteric plexus, a major nerve center for the gut, from age-related decline in functioning.[91] The myenteric plexus helps promote gut motility.

---

[86] Evid Based Complement Alternat Med. 2008 Mar; 5(1): 3–15.
[87] ibid
[88] Evid Based Complement Alternat Med. 2008 Mar; 5(1): 3–15.
[89] Oxid Med Cell Longev. 2014; 2014: 563179.
[90] Biomed Res Int. 2013; 2013: 469180.
[91] Evid Based Complement Alternat Med. 2015; 2015: 287153.

10. CORDYCEPS

Cordyceps sinensis (botanical name) may be the strangest kind of mushroom you ever run into, mainly because it's part caterpillar. No joke.

Despite sounding a little worrisome, cordyceps has a major reputation for improving health and vitality. There is much more research on cordyceps as compared to most other medicinal mushrooms.

Wild cordyceps mushrooms are formed when the cordyceps spores land on the caterpillar larvae of the Himalayan bat moth, found at high elevations in China, Tibet, Nepal and Bhutan. The mushroom grows inside the insect, consuming it from the inside. Once the insect is consumed and converted into a mushroom, the fruiting body is produced from the insect's head.

It's like the weirdest science fiction ever, except that it's real.

And rare. Extremely rare and over-harvested. Wild cordyceps costs over $20,000 per kilogram. At this point in time, almost no supplements contain wild cordyceps. Most contain a cordyceps product shown to have similar benefits without being grown on caterpillars.

Rather than caterpillars, the fungus is grown in a liquid nutrient solution. These products are considered the same as cordyceps and have been approved by the Chinese government as a safe and natural cordyceps product known as Cordyceps Cs-4. They still share the same botanical name as the original cordyceps (Cordyceps sinensis), despite being grown on liquid nutrients. There is functionally no difference between the wild type and manufactured cordyceps.

Cordyceps got its first modern news splash when it was credited with Chinese athletes breaking many records at the 1993 Chinese National Games. These athletes were later shown to be taking other performance enhancing drugs, so it is unclear what benefit cordyceps may have had. However, the mushroom was now well known.

Here are some of the benefits we know about cordyceps:

1. Cordyceps has an excellent reputation for athletic benefits.

    a. A group of athletes underwent high altitude training. Some took a combination cordyceps and Rhodiola crenulate (similar to the more popular rhodiola rosea), and some too a placebo. After 2 weeks of training, the group taking cordyceps and rhodiola showed improvements compared to the placebo group in two ways: first, they were able to run for a much longer time, and second, their parasympathetic activity decline (a measure of exhaustion) was prevented.[92]

    b. Cordyceps supplementation is associated with higher endurance performance, less fatigue and a higher metabolic threshold before lactic acid sets in.[93]

    c. Cordyceps improves cardiovascular responses in healthy runners, including enhancing heart rate variability[94], a characteristic that indicates better athletic performance as well as emotional stability.

2. Cordyceps helps regulate the immune system and is anti-inflammatory.[95]

3. Cordyceps may be neuroprotective. An extract appears to protect brain hippocampal cells from damage due to low oxygen conditions as well as protect against inflammation.[96]

4. In an animal study, cordyceps improved learning and memory impairment in mice who had received a drug that interferes with memory.[97]

[92] High Alt Med Biol. 2014 Sep;15(3):371-9. doi: 10.1089/ham.2013.1114.
[93] J Int Soc Sports Nutr. 2018; 15: 14.
[94] J Int Soc Sports Nutr. 2018; 15: 14.
[95] PLoS One. 2012;7(7):e40824. doi: 10.1371/journal.pone.004082
[96] Int J Med Mushrooms. 2015;17(9):829-40.
[97] Zhong Yao Cai. 2011 Sep;34(9):1403-5.

5. Another animal study examined the effect of cordyceps on aging and the brain. Results showed that cordyceps protected memory and learning abilities and significantly reduced oxidation damage.[98]

6. Cordyceps can help protect the mucosal gut barrier from toxin induced damage.[99]

7. Cordyceps may help patients with chronic kidney damage. A review of 22 studies showed that cordyceps helped decrease signs of kidney distress including serum creatinine and proteinuria.[100]

---

[98] Phytother Res. 2009 Jan;23(1):116-22. doi: 10.1002/ptr.2576.
[99] Int J Clin Exp Med. 2015 May 15;8(5):7333-41
[100] Cochrane Database Syst Rev. 2014 Dec 18;(12):CD008353.

Final note:

Mushrooms are amazing foods. They help continue the cycle of life by creating useful decay. They then convert that decay into food and into medicine. What a beautiful operation!

May we all see the value of this principle in our own lives and seek to convert the decay inherent to life into that which is good for us.

****